This book belongs
to

Amanda Furman

children's
choice

What Makes a Bird a Bird?

What makes
a bird
A BIRD?

by May Garelick

illustrated by Leonard Weisgard

 A Children's Choice® Book Club Edition From Scholastic Book Services

FOLLETT PUBLISHING COMPANY

ISBN 0-590-75759-8

In trees and in bushes, at the edge of a brook, on the ground, and in the air, birds are flying, singing, calling, bathing, nesting.

How do we know that a bird is a bird? What makes it a bird?

Is it a bird because it flies?

A fly flies. So do butterflies, ladybugs, dragonflies, and bees. But these are not birds. They
are insects.

Many insects fly. Not as fast as birds, not as
far as birds, but many insects fly.

And what is this, flying around in the middle
of the night?

It's not an insect.

It's not a bird.

It's a bat.

All day bats hang upside down, asleep in hollow
trees or in caves. At night they fly, catching
insects to eat as they fly around.

Bats fly, insects fly, birds fly, and other
things fly, too.

7

What do you think this is, flying above the water?

Is it a bat? An insect? A bird? No, it's a flying fish that has been frightened by an enemy under water. Like all fish, a flying fish lives most of the time in water. But if an enemy comes near, it can jump up out of the water, dart through the air, and escape.

Flying fish don't fly high and they don't fly far, but they fly higher and farther than some *birds*.

If there are flying insects, flying bats, and even flying fish, then it's not flying that makes a bird a bird.

As a matter of fact, you know a *bird* that doesn't fly.

Have you ever seen a chicken fly? Hardly ever.
Sometimes a chicken tries to fly. But it doesn't
get far. To get anywhere a chicken walks.
     Is a chicken a bird? Yes.

Another bird that doesn't fly is the ostrich.
It's the biggest bird in the world, but it can't fly. An ostrich can run fast, though — even faster than a horse. No wonder. Look at those long legs. That's why the ostrich is such a fast runner.

Can you think of another bird that can't fly?
A penguin can't fly. Penguins walk. Down to
the water they waddle, and into the sea for a swim.
If the ostrich can't fly, and penguins and
chickens can't fly, what makes them birds?
Are they birds because they have wings?

Birds have wings, all right. But look at a fly flying around. You can see its wings. And dragonflies and butterflies and bees have wings, too.

Not all insects have wings, but those that fly have to have wings. Anything that flies has to have wings.

Then what about a chicken and an ostrich? They have wings, but do not fly. Why? Their wings are too small to lift their bodies up in the air.

The penguin's little wings are like flippers. They're fine for swimming, but too small to lift the penguin up into the air.

Still an ostrich, a chicken, and a penguin are birds. So it isn't wings that make a bird a bird.

Is a bird a thing that sings?

Birds sing and call to each other, especially
in the spring. Some birds sing, some birds call,
some cluck, some quack. That's how birds talk to
each other.

One bird's song may mean, "This is my tree.
Keep away." Usually other birds do keep away.
If they don't, there's a fight.

"Chiree, chiree," a bird sings to a lady bird.
Maybe his song means, "Come join me."

A mother hen clucks to her chicks to tell them
that food is here.

"Cluck, cluck." And her baby chicks come running.

A duck quacks to her ducklings.

"Quack, quack." And her ducklings follow her.

"Peep, peep," call the baby robins.
And their parents know that the babies are hungry.

Birds sing and call messages to each other. But
singing and calling is not what makes a bird a bird.

Lots of *insects* sing and call their messages to
each other, too.

Crickets chirp, and grasshoppers hum. Katydids repeat their rhythmic song all night long. *Katydid, katydid, katy didn't.* And of all the insects, the tree cricket's song at night is the most beautiful. But these singers and callers are not birds. So it isn't singing that makes a bird a bird.

Then what *is* the special thing that makes a bird a bird?

Is it a bird if it builds a nest?

Birds build nests in trees, in bushes, under eaves, in barns. Sometimes they even build nests in mailboxes—wherever their eggs and their babies will be safe.

Birds' eggs must be kept warm in order to hatch. The nest and the mother's body keep the eggs warm.

But some birds build no nests at all. A whip-poorwill lays her eggs on the ground. But the eggs are the color of the ground around them— camouflaged—so they are safe.

The penguin that lives in the cold, icy Antarctic
builds no nest. The mother lays one egg. Then
the father penguin carries the egg on top of
his feet, close to his body. That's how he keeps
the egg warm for two months, until it is ready to
hatch.

Is this a bird's nest? It looks like one, doesn't it? But it isn't. It's a hornet's nest.

Other creatures make nests. Ants and bees, snakes and fish, and rabbits and mice make nests.

Nest building is not the special thing that makes a bird a bird.

Neither is egg-laying. All birds lay eggs, it's true. But so do frogs, snakes, fish, bees, mosquitoes, and many other creatures.

So—

It's not flying that makes a bird different
from anything else alive.

And it's not having wings.

And it's not singing or calling.

And it's not building nests or laying eggs.

What is it, then, that makes a bird a bird?

Birds have something that no other living thing has.

What is it?

FEATHERS!

Only birds have feathers. That's the special thing that makes a bird a bird. A bird has to have feathers to be a bird.

If it flies or not, if it sings or not; anything with feathers is a bird.

Feathers are strong. Try to break or tear one, and you'll see how strong a feather is. Bend a feather so the tip touches the bottom. Watch it spring back. It won't break.

Feathers are light. Hold a feather and you'll see how light it is. You've heard people say that something is "light as a feather."

Feathers are beautiful. They come in all colors. There are red cardinals, blue blue jays, black blackbirds, white doves, green parrots, brown sparrows, and many other colored birds in other colored feathers.

Feathers are useful, too.

They do many things for birds. Their flight feathers make birds the best flyers. Even though other creatures fly, no living creature can fly as long or as far as a bird.

A bird has several layers of feathers. There's a cloak of feathers that helps keep birds warm in winter. Watch a bird on a cold day. It looks like a fat puffball because it has fluffed out its feathers to keep out the cold.

A layer of flat feathers helps keep birds cool in summer. The heat from the bird's body works its way out through these feathers.

Feathers help keep birds dry in the rain. Put a drop of water on a feather, and watch the water slide off.

29

Birds take good care of their feathers. Some
birds bathe in water—ducking, splashing, spreading
their wings. Some birds bathe in fine dust. After
bathing, they preen their feathers carefully with
their beaks. From an oil sac at the tail, birds
take oil into their beaks to soften and straighten
their feathers.

But no matter how well birds clean their feathers, they get brittle and wear out. About once a year birds molt — their worn out feathers fall out. Not all at once, just one or two at a time. And as they fall out, new feathers grow in.

You may find some of these old feathers on the ground. Pick them up and look at them.

Feathers are the special things that *make a bird a bird.*

The Children's Choice® Clubhouse

It's the perfect place for playing or for curling up with a good book ★ Big enough to hold a few friends (it's 3′ x 4½′ and 4½′ tall) ★ Made of sturdy corrugated cardboard with a washable finish ★ Decorated inside and out with whimsical illustrations in full color ★ A very special gift.

To order, please send your name and address with a check or money order for $19.95 to:

Children's Choice® Clubhouse
Scholastic Inc.
900 Sylvan Ave.
Englewood Cliffs
New Jersey 07632